GENIUS

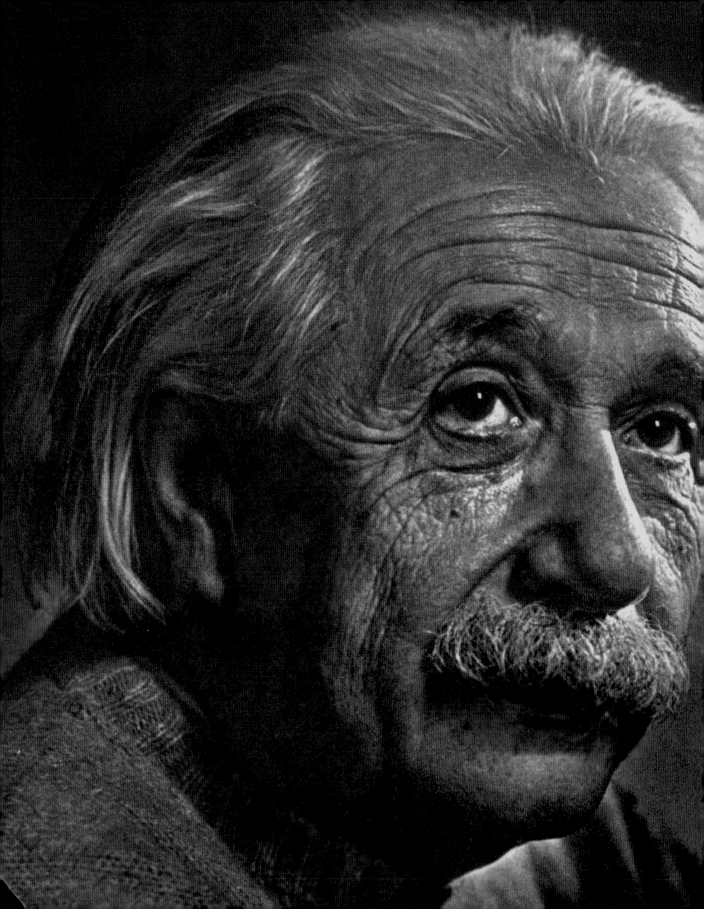

GENIUS

A PHOTOBIOGRAPHY OF ALBERT EINSTEIN

BY MARFÉ FERGUSON DELANO

NATIONAL GEOGRAPHIC

WASHINGTON, D.C.

For my husband, Geody Delano, and in memory of his mother,
Anne Kelsey Adriance—MFD

PUBLISHED BY THE
NATIONAL GEOGRAPHIC SOCIETY

John M. Fahey, Jr., President and Chief Executive Officer

Gilbert M. Grosvenor, Chairman of the Board

Nina D. Hoffman, Executive Vice President,
President of Books and Education Publishing Group

Ericka Markman, Senior Vice President, President
of Children's Books and Education Publishing Group

STAFF FOR THIS BOOK

Nancy Laties Feresten, Vice President, Editor-in-Chief, Children's Books

Bea Jackson, Art Director, Children's Books

Jennifer Emmett, Project Editor

Marty Ittner, Designer

Stephanie Maze, Illustrations Editor

Janet Dustin, Illustrations Coordinator

Susan Kehnemui Donnelly, Editorial Assistant

Carl Mehler, Director of Maps

Nicholas P. Rosenbach, Map Research

Gregory Ugiansky, Map Production

Mark A. Wentling, Indexer

R. Gary Colbert, Production Director

Lewis R. Bassford, Production Manager

Vincent P. Ryan, Manufacturing Manager

Library of Congress Cataloging-in-Publication Data

Delano, Marfé Ferguson.
  Genius: A Photobiography of Albert Einstein / by Marfé Ferguson Delano.
    p. cm.
  Trade Edition ISBN 0-7922-9544-7;   Library Edition ISBN 0-7922-9545-5
1. Einstein, Albert, 1879–1955—Pictorial works. 2. Physicists—Biography. I. Title.
  QC16.E5D45 2005
  530'.092—dc22
  2004015001

ACKNOWLEDGMENTS

The author and the publisher gratefully acknowledge the generous help of the staff of the Albert Einstein Archives of the Jewish National & University Library at the Hebrew University of Jerusalem, Israel, for their review of the text and layout. Thanks also to Joseph Serene, Professor of Physics, Georgetown University, for his scientific review.

The author thanks her wonderful editor, Jennifer Emmett, as well as Suzanne Fonda, Nancy Feresten, Bea Jackson, and Janet Dustin for their encouragement and expertise. Special thanks to Marty Ittner for her inspired book design. To my children and husband, a huge thank-you for reviewing countless revisions of the sections on relativity. Your comments really helped. Finally, thanks to my sister Sherri for letting me off the hook so graciously. You're the best.

The body text of the book is set in Mrs. Eaves.

The display text is set in UV39, DuChirico, and Officina Sans.

FRONT COVER: Albert Einstein in 1941. A manuscript handwritten by the scientist in 1946 appears in the background.

BACK COVER: In response to a photographer's request for a "birthday pose" on his 72nd birthday, Einstein jokingly sticks out his tongue.

HALF-TITLE PAGE: This detail from a letter written by Einstein features his famous equation, $E=mc^2$, in his own hand.

TITLE PAGE: Einstein in a reflective mood.

OPPOSITE PAGE: Visiting a friend in California in 1933, Einstein takes a bicycle for a spin.

"One thing I have learned in a long life; that all our science, measured against reality, is primitive and childlike—and yet it is the most precious thing we have."

At his 70th birthday celebration at his Princeton home in 1949, Albert Einstein visits with Jewish refugee children who survived the Holocaust. This photograph was taken by Philippe Halsman, himself a refugee whom Einstein had helped come to America nine years earlier. The manuscript in the background, written in Einstein's own hand, discusses the general theory of relativity.

FOREWORD

My time with Albert Einstein, my grandfather, passed all too quickly. He died when I was 14, and our time together when he was alive was limited, too. We didn't live in the same place—he in Princeton, New Jersey, and I in California or Switzerland.

But I remember that when we did spend time together, it was always on an equal playing field. He never condescended or talked down. Rather than expecting me to become a miniature adult for the encounter, what he did was throw himself into being a child with me. In that, he was like no other adult I knew. I think it was this talent of his to retain the child within himself that aided him in his scientific pursuits. He never lost his childlike awe of the universe, nor did he feel restricted by having to behave like an adult. He could let his mind range freely and sometimes ask preposterous-seeming questions, which ultimately led to elegant answers. Both he and I shared an insatiable curiosity, which I think comes from the realm of childhood. We corresponded until his death, and he always encouraged my curiosity about the universe and challenged my thinking and outlook.

Albert Einstein was not only a brilliant thinker, he was also a warm and gentle man, a true humanist. In my life, I've treasured my grandfather's legacy of kindness and care for others and his love of music and nature, and, above all, sailing. I have been told that he was impressed by my own love of sailing as a very small child. From his example, I learned to love and seek peacefulness in a sailboat—the gentle lapping of the waves, the hoarse bark of the sea lions, the screech of gulls, and the flapping of sails. This is one of the most peaceful feelings I know.

It's a wonderful thing to share the memory of someone you love with others. I hope the story of Albert Einstein's scientific and humanitarian achievements will be as inspiring to you as my own memories of a warm, funny, and thoughtful grandfather are to me.

Evelyn Einstein

—Evelyn Einstein

ALBERT EINSTEIN MIGHT HAVE SMILED at the title of this book. He found it amusing that people considered him a genius. Although he was proud of his achievements, he saw himself as just an ordinary person. In fact, he once said, "I have no special talents. I am only passionately curious." Yet if anyone deserves to be labeled a genius, it is Albert Einstein. His ideas not only laid the path for much of 20th-century science, they remain vital to science in this century as well. His masterpiece, called the general theory of relativity, brought him worldwide fame. It also transformed our everyday ideas of time and space and the way the universe works.

Albert Einstein was born on March 14, 1879, in Ulm, a small city in southern Germany. He was the first child of Hermann and Pauline Koch Einstein, a middle-class Jewish couple. As a high-school student, Hermann had shown a knack for math. But his family could not afford to send him to university, so he became a businessman. He worked as a featherbed salesman at the time of Albert's birth. Albert would later describe his father as "exceedingly friendly, mild, and wise." Eleven years younger than her husband, Pauline was a strong-willed woman who came from a well-to-do family. She loved music and was a talented pianist.

According to family legend, when Albert was a newborn his head looked so big and strange that his mother feared he might be deformed. Then when he reached the age at which most children begin to speak,

Albert Einstein was three years old when this portrait was made. As a child he preferred puzzles and building blocks to rowdy games.

"When I was a little boy my father showed me a small compass, and the enormous impression that it made on me certainly played a role in my life."

Albert, about 14 years old here, sits for the camera with his sister, Maja.

Albert made no attempts to do so. He later recalled, "My parents were worried because I began to speak fairly late, so that they even consulted a doctor." They need not have feared. When Albert was between two and three years old, he finally started to speak, much to his parents' relief.

The Einsteins moved to Munich, Germany, in 1880. Hermann went into business with his brother Jakob, an engineer who was starting an electrical contracting company in the bustling city. In November 1881, Albert's younger sister, Maja, was born. When he first saw her, he is said to have asked, "Where are its wheels?" He had been expecting a toy, not a baby. But if he felt disappointment, it did not last. Albert soon adored Maja, and she remained his closest friend all her life.

Maja later recalled that as a young boy Albert enjoyed playing by himself with building blocks. He also liked to build houses of cards and once constructed one that was 14 stories high. Albert and his sister occasionally fought, as siblings will do. Sometimes when he was mad he threw things at her. Once it was a bowling ball. Another time he smacked her on the head with a hoe. Maja later joked that "it takes a sound skull to be the sister of an intellectual."

Hermann and Pauline Einstein were loving parents who encouraged their children's independence and curiosity. Albert was not much older than four when his mother allowed him to walk alone through the busy streets of Munich. (She secretly followed him to make sure he could handle it.)

Pauline also shared her passion for music with her children. Around the age of five, Albert began violin lessons. He was not wild about practicing, but his mother insisted, so he stuck with it. Looking back many years later, Albert said that he "really began to learn [to play the violin] only when I was about 13 years old, mainly after I had fallen in love with Mozart's sonatas." From then on he loved the violin, and music brought him joy throughout his life.

The same year Albert began violin his father showed him a magnetic compass. It filled the boy with wonder. He saw with excitement that no matter which way the compass was turned, the needle always pointed north, as if guided by

Albert's parents are shown here in front of a busy Munich street scene. Pauline Einstein was a strict but loving mother who encouraged her son's musical talents. Hermann Einstein was a kind-hearted man who unfortunately had little success in business.

an invisible force. Later he would say, "I can still remember—or at least believe I can remember—that this experience made a deep and lasting impression upon me. Something deeply hidden had to be behind things."

Although the Einsteins were of Jewish ancestry, they were not particularly religious. When the time came for Albert to start school, they enrolled him in a nearby Catholic elementary school, which was closer to their home as well as less expensive than the local Jewish school. (Because religious instruction was required by the city of Munich, he was tutored in the Jewish faith by a distant relative at home.) Contrary to rumors that persist to this day, young Albert was not a poor student. He actually did quite well. A letter written by Pauline to her mother in 1886 noted with pride, "Yesterday Albert got his grades, once again he was ranked first, he got a splendid report card."

In this 1889 class photograph from the Luitpold-Gymnasium, Albert is third from right in the first row. He detested the teaching methods at the German schools he attended, where students were expected to recite facts without taking time to think things through.

ALBERT EINSTEIN IN CENTRAL EUROPE

This map shows places in Europe where Einstein lived. He was born in Ulm, Germany; then his family moved to Munich. He joined them in Milan, Italy, in 1894. He attended high school in Aarau, Switzerland, and university in Zurich. He later lived in Bern, Prague, and Berlin. In 1933 Einstein moved to the United States. He never returned to Europe.

Despite getting good grades, Albert didn't really like school. Like most German schools of the time, the one he attended was very strict and emphasized rote learning, which is based on memorizing facts and figures. Albert liked to think for himself, not be told what to think. Moreover, discipline at the school could be harsh. For example, if a student answered slowly or incorrectly, a teacher might rap him on the hand with a ruler. Looking back on his school years, Einstein noted, "To me the worst thing seems to be for a school principally to work with the methods of fear, force, and artificial authority. Such treatment destroys the sound sentiments, the sincerity, and the self-confidence of the pupil."

When he was nine, Albert transferred from the elementary school to the Luitpold-Gymnasium, a school that prepared students for university study. To his dismay, it was even more rigid and militaristic than his old school. He did not put much effort into subjects that bored him, such as Greek, and this attitude irritated some of his teachers. One of them is said to have declared in front of the whole class that Albert would never amount to anything.

By the age of 14, when this portrait was taken, Albert was fascinated by math and physics.

Albert excelled at math and science, however, because they fascinated him. Indeed, so great was his curiosity about these subjects that he began to study them on his own when he was about ten. With support from family and friends, he soon advanced far beyond the level of study at his school. He pored over popular books on science with "breathless attention." Physics, the science that deals with energy, matter, and movement, particularly intrigued him.

Nudged along by his Uncle Jakob, Albert taught himself algebra. When he was 12 or so he received a geometry textbook from a family friend. He later spoke of it as a "holy book" because of the powerful effect it had on his imagination. He worked his way through the book in a few months, then tackled higher math, including calculus. He also read books on philosophy.

When Albert was 15, his world turned upside down. His family decided to move to Milan, Italy—without him. Hermann and Jakob's company had fallen on hard times, and the brothers decided to seek better luck in Italy. Hermann decided that it would be best for Albert to finish his education at the Luitpold-Gymnasium. Plans were made for the teenager to stay with a distant relative in Munich.

Albert was miserable without his parents and Maja. He had few friends at school. Classmates called him "Biedermeier," which roughly translates as "Honest John." That's like being called a "nerd" today. Moreover, Albert continued to displease his teachers because he did not even try to hide his boredom and his contempt for what he called their "dull, mechanized method of teaching." After a lonely six months on his own, Albert could stand it no longer. He dropped out of school, packed his violin, and took a train to Italy. The Gymnasium, for its part, was not sorry to see him go.

Albert had another reason to leave Germany when he did. If he left before his 17th birthday, he could avoid the military service German law required of all males. But if he left after he turned 17 and did not report back for duty, he would be declared a deserter.

Their son's arrival surprised and concerned Hermann and Pauline Einstein. He reassured them that he was not abandoning his education. Through independent study, he said, he would prepare himself for entrance to a university. Albert had another important decision to share with his parents. He announced that he disliked the nation of his birth so much he had decided to give up, or renounce, his German citizenship. Einstein later explained that "the over-emphasized military mentality in the German State was alien to me even as a boy." Because he was still a minor the law did not allow him to make the change on his own. So he talked his father into filing the required papers on his behalf.

The spring and summer of 1895 were among the happiest times of Albert's life. Instead of going to school, he spent time with his family, hiked in the mountains, visited friends in the Italian countryside, and explored art museums and churches. He relished his independence and studied the subjects he loved. He also made time to write a scientific essay, which he sent to his favorite uncle, Caesar Koch, his mother's brother. In it he outlined his ideas about electricity and magnetism.

In the fall of 1895, 16-year-old Albert headed over the Alps to Zurich, in the German-speaking part of Switzerland. He had convinced his parents to let him apply to the Swiss Federal Institute of Technology, commonly called the Polytechnic. Full of confidence—even though he was two years younger than most candidates for admission—he took the entrance exam. He failed it. Although his math and science scores were outstanding, he flunked languages and history. Still, there was hope. The director of the Polytechnic was impressed by Albert's remarkable mathematical abilities. He advised him to attend a highly regarded Swiss high school in the nearby town of Aarau for a year and then reapply.

To Albert's joy the school in Aarau differed greatly from the Luitpold-Gymnasium. The atmosphere was open and friendly, and the teachers encouraged students to think freely rather than just parrot facts. Moreover, it had an excellent physics lab. Albert was popular with his classmates, one of whom remembered him as "sure of himself" and "unhampered by convention." One day at school Albert played the violin for his friends and surprised them with the beauty and "fire...in his playing."

Albert thrived during the year he spent at Aarau, and his interest in physics blossomed. He was particularly fascinated by the nature of light. Thinking about it led to what he called his first "thought experiment."

Albert treasured the months he spent playing hooky from school and roaming around northern Italy in 1895. He especially liked hiking in the Italian Alps, pictured here under a layer of snow.

"The happy months of my stay in Italy
are very beautiful memories....
Days and weeks without anxiety and tension."

Seated at left in the front row, Albert poses with classmates from the high school in Aarau, Switzerland. It was in Aarau that he embarked on his first thought experiments about the nature of light.

"What if one were to run after a ray of light?
...What if one were riding on the beam?
...If one were to run fast enough, would
it no longer move at all?"

What would it be like, he wondered, if you could ride on a beam of light? He was to ponder the question for ten years before he found the answer.

In January 1896 Albert received the official notice ending his German citizenship. For the next five years he was not a citizen of any country. Later in 1896 Albert graduated from the high school in Aarau with high marks and was accepted at the Polytechnic.

In the fall Albert rented a room in Zurich and entered the Swiss Federal Institute of Technology. His father urged him to study electrical engineering, so that he might perhaps one day join the family business. Albert had another idea in mind. He decided to study physics and mathematics, with the aim of becoming a teacher of those subjects.

After a few months at the Polytechnic, Albert fell back into his old habits. He neglected the subjects that did not interest him, and he cut classes more often than he attended them. He even skipped physics, because the professor refused to teach the latest theories. To Einstein, physics was a living science full of puzzles waiting to be solved, not just an established set of rules. So he studied it on his own, reading science journals to keep up on the latest theories.

In his four years at the Polytechnic, Einstein also spent a lot of time at coffeehouses, where he loved to discuss science and philosophy and art and literature with friends. He was a hit at parties, where he entertained guests with his violin playing. Einstein later recalled that during this time he experienced "a freedom which I thoroughly enjoyed...up to a few months before the examination." That was when he realized that he had to catch up on everything he had missed in school over the years if he wanted to graduate.

Einstein crammed for the exam using the excellent class notes taken by his good friend Marcel Grossmann. Thanks in no small part to those notes, Einstein passed. He received his degree in 1900, but he was so burned out from having to "cram all this stuff" into his mind for the exam that he found "the consideration of any scientific problems distasteful...for a year."

After graduation Einstein tried to find a teaching or research position in physics. He applied to several universities but they all turned him down. This happened in part because he lacked a proper letter of recommendation from the Polytechnic. His cocky attitude and failure to show up for class had annoyed the faculty. "From what people tell me," he wrote, "I am not in the good graces of any of my former teachers."

Einstein badly needed work. Now that he was out of college he was on his own financially. To make ends meet, he took temporary jobs. He worked as a private tutor and as a substitute high school teacher. Gradually his passion for science returned. He wrote a research article on the theory of liquids that was published in an important German scientific journal called the *Annalen der Physik* in 1901. That same year

Einstein (*top, at right*) sits with Marcel Grossmann. The two met as students at the Swiss Federal Institute of Technology in Zurich (*bottom*), and they became lifelong friends. Grossmann's excellent notes helped the class-cutting Einstein pass his final exams. In the background is Einstein's school-leaving certificate from the high school he attended in Aarau.

"I'm so lucky to have found you, a creature who is my equal, and who is as strong and independent as I am."

Fellow student Mileva Maric's dark eyes and bright mind captured Einstein's heart. He called her his "Doxerl," which means "little doll." The quotation above is taken from one of the many love letters he wrote to her, one of which is displayed here behind a picture of the couple taken in Prague in 1912.

Einstein became a Swiss citizen. And he continued to romance a dark-eyed young woman from Serbia named Mileva Maric.

Einstein had fallen in love with Mileva when they were both physics students at the Polytechnic. Few women studied science at that time, and she intrigued him. Four years older than Einstein, Mileva was shy, serious, and very smart. She shared his love of music, math, and physics. He often discussed his new scientific ideas with her, and sometimes she helped him with mathematical calculations. They decided to marry. Albert's parents, however, opposed the match. His mother thought Mileva was too old for her son, and she also looked down on her for being Serbian.

Despite his parents' disapproval, Albert promised he would marry Mileva once he landed a full-time job. Before that happened, however, Mileva became pregnant. Because Albert could not yet afford to support a family, the couple did not marry. Mileva returned to her parents' home in Serbia, where she gave birth to a baby girl in early 1902. From the few records that mention her, the child appears to have been given up for adoption or to have died in early childhood. Einstein never met his daughter. Mileva grieved over the loss of her child for the rest of her life.

In the summer of 1902 Einstein finally found a steady job. Thanks to a recommendation from the father of his friend Marcel Grossmann, Einstein was hired by the Swiss Patent Office. Located in the capital city of Bern, it was a government agency that issued patents. (Patents are official documents that give a person or company the sole right to make or sell an invention.) As a technical expert third class, Einstein reviewed proposals for inventions to decide whether they might actually work.

Proud parents, Mileva and Einstein show off their firstborn son, Hans Albert.

That fall Hermann Einstein died. On his deathbed he consented to his son's marriage. In January 1903 Albert and Mileva were wed in Bern. Not long after their marriage, Einstein wrote to a friend, "Well, now I am a married man and am living a very pleasant, cozy life with my wife. She takes excellent care of everything, cooks well, and is always cheerful." The couple's first son, Hans Albert, was born in 1904.

Einstein enjoyed his job at the patent office. The work was challenging enough to be interesting, but he still had plenty of time and energy to concentrate on his own scientific research. Visitors to the Einstein home were likely to find him "sitting…in front of a heap of papers covered with mathematical formulas…writing with his right hand and holding his…son in his left."

This bird's-eye view shows Bern, Switzerland, as it looked a century ago. Einstein lived there from 1902 to 1909.

In 1905 the new ideas about physics that had been simmering in Einstein's brain bubbled over. In a period of less than eight months, while working six full days a week at the patent office, the 26-year-old published four articles in the *Annalen der Physik* that revolutionized science. He did this without access to a laboratory. His only tools were paper, pencil, and his incredible imagination.

The first of these articles had to do with the structure of light—a topic that had long been on Einstein's mind. He was partly inspired by the work of Scottish scientist James Clerk Maxwell, who had shown in the 1860s that light is a type of electromagnetic wave. (Electromagnetic waves are composed of both electric and magnetic fields.) Einstein was also intrigued by research that German physicist Max Planck had conducted in 1900. Planck's work suggested that heat and light given off by a hot object are emitted and absorbed in distinct packets of energy. He called these packets "quanta."

Einstein respected Maxwell's work on the wave theory of light. But he didn't let that limit his imagination. Using Planck's quantum idea as a starting point, the young patent clerk proposed that light consists of a stream of packets, or particles, which he dubbed light quanta. We now call these particles photons. Then he used this quantum theory of light to explain a phenomenon called the photoelectric effect. This occurs when a beam of light hits certain metals and causes them to give off electrically charged particles called electrons. Simply put, Einstein

This portrait of Einstein at the Swiss Patent Office was taken in 1905—the same year he produced four groundbreaking articles that revolutionized science.

showed that photons in the light beam knock the electrons out of the metal.

Einstein's explanation of the photoelectric effect eventually helped lay the foundation for a new branch of science called quantum physics. That in turn helped pave the way for much of today's technology, including television, lasers, remote-control devices, and computer chips.

The young patent clerk's second breakthrough paper dealt with atoms and molecules. Today we take the existence of these tiny particles for granted. We learn in school that atoms and molecules—which are made up of one or more atoms—are the building blocks of all matter, from air to feathers to people. At the turn of the 20th century, however, the existence of atoms and molecules was merely suspected, not confirmed.

Einstein set out to prove that atoms and molecules are real things. He did this by calculating how a microscopic particle suspended in a liquid—a grain of pollen in water, for example—ought to move if atoms in the liquid kept banging it around. It turned out that the zigzagging motion his equations predicted was identical with the way such particles actually do move. This movement, called Brownian motion after the Scottish botanist who first described it in 1827, had long been noticed by scientists. But they were unable to explain it until Einstein's paper came along. His calculations convinced them that Brownian motion is caused by the movement of atoms, and that therefore atoms and molecules really do exist.

Einstein's most startling idea was still to come. In his third and

fourth major papers of 1905, he tackled the question he had been pondering since he was 16: What would you see if you could hitch a ride on a beam of light? Thinking about this led him to the special theory of relativity, which overturned traditional physics.

At the time, the accepted view of how the universe worked was the one that English scientist Isaac Newton had established more than 200 years earlier. In his 1687 book, *Principia Mathematica,* Newton introduced three laws of motion and a theory of gravity, all of which he expressed in mathematical equations. His theory of gravity said that a force called gravity acts between every pair of objects in the universe and pulls them

Einstein credited four men for laying the foundations on which he built his special theory of relativity. Shown left to right, they are Italian scientist Galileo Galilei (1564–1642); English scientist Isaac Newton (1642–1727); Scottish scientist James Clerk Maxwell (1831–1879); and Dutch scientist Hendrik Antoon Lorentz (1835–1928), whom Einstein came to know as a friend and colleague.

toward each other. Together with his laws of motion, it explained the movements of objects in the heavens—such as planets and stars—as well as those on Earth. Newton assumed that these movements took place against a background where time and space were fixed, or absolute. In other words, time ticked by at the same rate for everyone, and distances measured the same for all observers.

In his article on special relativity, Einstein proposed that all observers measure the same speed of light, regardless of whether they're moving toward the source of light or away from it. But that seemed impossible. Everyday experience tells us that speed is relative. That is, it varies according to the motion of an observer. For example, if you're on a train traveling 40 miles per hour and you throw a baseball at 20 miles per hour in the same direction that the train is moving, to you the ball would look as if it were moving at 20 miles per hour. But to a person standing by the tracks watching the train go by, the ball would seem to be whizzing by at 60 miles per hour. So how could the speed of light possibly seem the same to observers who were moving at different speeds?

To solve the puzzle, Einstein ignored everyday experience and tossed aside Newton's ideas about fixed time and space. He realized that for the speed of light to stay the same, then something else would have to give. And that gave him the key to his thought experiment: If he could travel near the speed of light, then time and distance would appear one way to him and another way to someone moving at a different speed. Time and space, Einstein declared, are not absolute; they are relative to the observer.

The universe, according to Einstein, was not quite what everybody had thought for more than 200 years. Time didn't tick by at the same rate for everyone. This led to the astonishing prediction that the faster an object moves, the slower time passes for it compared to an observer at rest. The idea may seem crazy at first. But that's because in normal life everything moves far too slowly for us to ever notice this effect. Einstein's theory has been confirmed by experiments. In one of them, researchers flew an extremely accurate atomic clock around the world in a high-speed jet. Compared to an identical clock that had stayed in place on Earth, the clock that flew on the jet ticked slower.

A few months after introducing his special theory of relativity, Einstein added a new twist to it. More thought on the subject had led him to the extraordinary idea that mass (the physical stuff of the universe) and energy are different forms of the same thing. He later summed up this relationship in what has become the most famous equation ever: $E=mc^2$, or Energy (E) equals mass (m) multiplied by the speed of light (c) squared (^{2}). The speed of light is approximately 186,000 miles per second (300,000 kilometers per second). If you square this figure, which

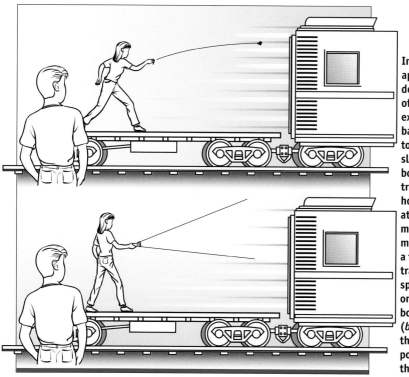

In everyday life speed appears to vary depending on the motion of the observer. For example, if a girl throws a ball on a train, it appears to her to be moving slower than it does to a boy watching from the tracks (*top*). Light, however, always travels at the same speed, no matter how an observer is moving. So the beam from a flashlight seems to travel at the same speed to both the girl on the train and to the boy on the tracks (*bottom*). Einstein used this fact as a starting point for his special theory of relativity.

"Imagination is more important than knowledge. Knowledge is limited, imagination encircles the world."

means multiplying it by itself, you get an incredibly large number. So in essence what the equation says is that there is a vast amount of energy bound up in a tiny amount of mass. (Some 30 years later, other scientists would develop ways to unleash this energy and create nuclear weapons.)

Besides producing the groundbreaking articles described above, Einstein also completed his doctoral thesis and earned his Ph.D. degree from Zurich University in 1905. Indeed, so amazing were his achievements that year that it came to be called his *annus mirabilis,* which is Latin for "year of wonders."

Word of Einstein's articles soon spread among physicists. In particular, his special theory of relativity sparked lively discussion. Some scientists were skeptical of it, but many others grasped it as the solution to physics problems they had been puzzling over. In the meantime, Einstein continued to work at the patent office and to think about the mysteries of the universe in his spare time. He published more papers about physics. And in 1909 he finally landed a teaching job. The University of Zurich hired him as a professor of theoretical physics, and the Einstein family moved to Zurich.

In 1910 Mileva gave birth to their second son, Eduard. The following year Einstein accepted a better-paying position at the German University in the Czech city of Prague. The family packed up and moved again, but they didn't stay in Prague for long. Einstein's fame as a brilliant scientist had grown, and several institutions wanted him on their faculty. In 1912 the Zurich Polytechnic—where Einstein had once failed the entrance exam—lured the young scientist to their staff, and the family returned to Zurich.

A student whom Einstein tutored in Bern in 1905 said that the scientist's "striking brown eyes radiate deeply and softly. His voice is attractive, like the vibrant note of a cello." This portrait of Einstein was made in 1921.

"I sometimes ask myself how did it come that I was the one to develop the theory of relativity. The reason, I think, is that a normal adult never stops to think about problems of space and time. These are things which he has thought of as a child. But...I began to wonder about space and time only when I had already grown up."

By 1912, about the time this photograph was taken, Einstein had earned a reputation as a brilliant scientist. Nobel Prize–winning physicist Marie Curie, who discovered radium, remarked on "the clarity of his mind, the breadth of his information, and the profundity of his knowledge." Einstein's special theory of relativity continued to excite debate about space and time, and scientists around the world pondered the implications of his famous equation, $E=mc^2$. In the background, a detail from a letter written in Einstein's own hand shows that the E in the equation was originally an L. Einstein used L to symbolize energy until 1912, when he switched to the letter E.

Although he was popular with his students, now that he was a professor Einstein found that teaching didn't really suit him. It took so long to prepare for lectures that he had less time for his original research than he'd had in his patent office days. So when the University of Berlin in Germany asked him to be the director of a new institute of physics and offered him a research position without teaching duties, he was very tempted. Moreover, the job would give him the chance to talk trade with some of Europe's top scientists. So he accepted the offer, despite his misgivings about returning to Germany. He still didn't trust its military mindset.

In the spring of 1914, the Einstein family left Switzerland for Berlin. It would be Einstein's home for the next 18 years. Mileva and the boys stayed for only a few months.

In 1911 Einstein (*standing, far right*) attended the world's first physics conference, known as the Solvay Congress, in Brussels, Belgium. Other participants included Marie Curie (*seated, second from right*) and Hendrik Antoon Lorentz (*seated, fourth from left*).

This picture of Mileva with Eduard (*left*) and Hans Albert was taken around the time she and Einstein separated. Einstein asked her to "send me news of my precious boys every two weeks."

Over the past couple of years, Albert and Mileva's marriage had grown unhappy. He gave more time to his science than to his family, and she complained of being "starved for love." Mileva had not wanted to move to Berlin in the first place, and once she got there she hated it. To make things worse, Albert had become romantically involved with his cousin Elsa Loewenthal, a divorced woman who lived in Berlin with her two daughters. That summer Albert and Mileva decided to separate.

Mileva took Hans Albert and Eduard back with her to Switzerland. Einstein saw them off at the station, then cried the rest of the day. Although he no longer loved his wife, he adored his two sons, whom he called his "little bears." In the years that followed, he kept in touch with them through letters and holiday visits. For the most part, Einstein was content to let Mileva raise the children so that he could concentrate on his work. Hans Albert eventually became a professor of engineering in California. Eduard, a talented pianist, developed mental illness as a young man and spent the rest of his life in and out of a psychiatric hospital.

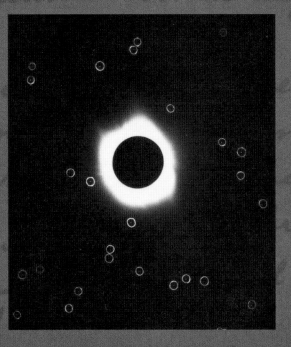

"I occupy myself exclusively with the problem of gravitation....Compared with this problem, the original theory of relativity is child's play."

During the solar eclipse of 1919, British astronomers took photographs that confirmed Einstein's prediction that starlight should bend when it passes through the sun's gravitational field. This photograph is from the eclipse of 1922, when astronomers reconfirmed the effect. In the letter in the background, Einstein discusses this effect and sketches out his idea.

In August 1914 World War I broke out, and Germany was in the middle of it. The German public's enthusiasm for the war disgusted Einstein. He couldn't understand how people could cheer soldiers marching off to war. And he was outraged when 93 leading German intellectuals signed a manifesto, or declaration, defending Germany's aggressive war conduct. A few days later, Einstein and three others signed an antiwar manifesto. Einstein began to speak publicly in favor of pacifism—the view that war and violence are morally unacceptable ways of settling conflict.

During the war years, however, he devoted most of his energy to his research. In 1915 he wrote to Hans Albert that "I have just completed the most splendid work of my life." Ever since his special theory of relativity was published, Einstein had been troubled that it didn't take gravity into account. Then in 1907, he recalled, "I was sitting in the patent office in Bern when all of a sudden a thought occurred to me: if a person falls freely, he won't feel his own weight. I was startled. This simple thought...impelled me toward a theory of gravitation."

It took Einstein another eight years to sort out his new theory. He wrote a friend that "every step is devilishly difficult." His reliable friend Marcel Grossmann, now a mathematics professor, helped him find the mathematical tools he needed to work out his ideas. In the March 1916 issue of the *Annalen der Physik* Einstein finally published his masterpiece, "The Foundation of the General Theory of Relativity."

According to Einstein, space and time are joined together to form something called spacetime. Put very simply, the general theory of relativity says that gravity is what happens when spacetime is bent, or warped, by matter.

To make this concept easier to understand, spacetime is often compared to a trampoline with a bowling ball resting on it. The ball (matter) causes the trampoline to bend and sag. If you try to roll a marble across the trampoline, instead of going in a straight line it curves down toward the dip caused by the bowling ball. If you roll the marble just right, it will circle, or orbit, the bowling ball. The sun bends spacetime in a similar way. Earth and the other planets go around the sun just as the marble goes around the bowling ball. This effect is what we call gravity.

Einstein used his new theory to predict that starlight should bend when it passed by the sun. This could be proved, he said, during a solar eclipse. That's when the moon's shadow falls on the Earth and blocks out the sun's rays for a little while. With the sun's glare out of the way, light from stars beyond the sun can be seen and measured. British astronomers tested Einstein's prediction during a total eclipse of the sun in May 1919.

That same year, Einstein finally obtained a divorce from Mileva. He married his cousin Elsa a few months later and moved into the comfortable apartment she shared with her two daughters. Although Elsa didn't even try to understand his work, she had a warm and

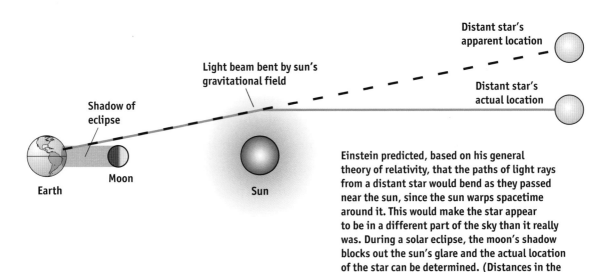

Distant star's apparent location

Light beam bent by sun's gravitational field

Distant star's actual location

Shadow of eclipse

Earth

Moon

Sun

Einstein predicted, based on his general theory of relativity, that the paths of light rays from a distant star would bend as they passed near the sun, since the sun warps spacetime around it. This would make the star appear to be in a different part of the sky than it really was. During a solar eclipse, the moon's shadow blocks out the sun's glare and the actual location of the star can be determined. (Distances in the diagram are not to scale.)

In high spirits, Einstein and his second wife, Elsa, set sail for America in 1921. By this time word of his amazing theories had spread around the world.

motherly personality that suited him. She enjoyed taking care of him, and he enjoyed being taken care of.

In November 1919 the results obtained during the eclipse were published. Einstein was right: The starlight bent at the angle he had predicted. His general theory of relativity was confirmed. Contrary to Newton's view, space and time weren't merely the background of the universe. Together they formed spacetime, which affects the path of anything moving through it, from the planets to rays of light. And gravity wasn't a force in the way that Newton believed; it was the effect of the bending of spacetime by matter.

The news created a sensation among scientists and ordinary people alike. Headlines in the next day's *London Times* declared "Revolution in

French Government to Open
Cheap National Restaurant

PARIS, Nov. 9.—

The American public hailed Albert Einstein as a hero when he paid his first visit to the United States in 1921. In New York, thousands of fans lined the streets as his motorcade (*left*) drove to City Hall, where he was welcomed by the mayor. Einstein returned to the U.S. ten years later, more popular than ever. Movie star Charlie Chaplin invited the scientist to attend the opening of his film *City Lights* in Los Angeles (*below, right*). During this visit, the Einsteins also traveled to the Grand Canyon, where they visited with Hopi Indians (*below, left*). The *New York Times* article in the background broke the story of Einstein's amazing new theory of the universe in November 1919.

Stars Not Where They Seemed

A BOOK

of His Flight Their Views
on Right of Asylum.

NO DEMAND FOR HIM

Negotiations with Belgium
Territorial Adjustments

Science…New Theory of the Universe…Newtonian Ideas Overthrown."
A couple days later the *New York Times* spread the word: "Lights All Askew in
the Heavens…Einstein's Theory Triumphs: Stars Not Where They Seemed."
The 40-year-old scientist became a celebrity practically overnight.

Einstein's general theory of relativity thrilled the public. Not many
people understood what it meant at first, but that didn't matter. It was
enough to know that someone had come up with a totally new explanation of the universe. People were still weary from the First World War,
which had just ended, and they were longing for good news.

People were as fascinated by Einstein the man as they were by his
mind-boggling ideas. The friendly, carelessly dressed scientist with
a gentle manner and wild hair charmed them. The press seized on his
every word and reported his every move. Einstein felt "flooded with
questions, invitations, and suggestions" from admirers. He liked the
attention at first, but he soon came to miss his privacy. As he wrote to
a friend, "Just as with the man in the fairy tale who turned whatever he
touched into gold, with me everything is turned to newspaper clamor."

Einstein was surprised but pleased at the widespread interest in his
new theory. In 1920 he commented to his friend Marcel Grossmann,
"At present every coachman and every waiter argues about whether or
not the relativity theory is correct."

Not everyone admired Einstein, however. Many Germans already dis-
trusted him because he had spoken out in favor of pacifism and world
government during the war, which Germany lost. The fact that he was a
Jew made some people trust him even less. Prejudice and hatred against
Jews—known as anti-Semitism—were on the rise in Germany. Some anti-
Semitic scientists attacked Einstein's theory of relativity as "Jewish physics."

In reaction to the increased anti-Semitism, Einstein began to identify
more strongly with his Jewish roots and to support Jewish causes.
He proudly proclaimed, "The pursuit of knowledge for its own sake,

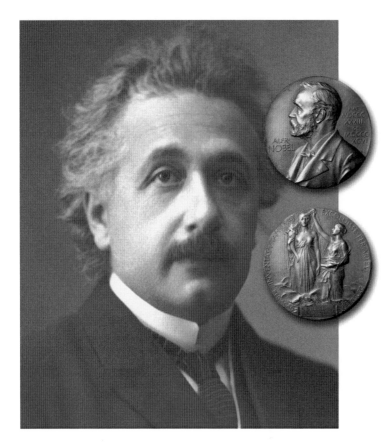

Einstein, shown here in his official Nobel portrait, received the 1921 Nobel Prize for Physics. He was awarded a gold medal, the front and back of which are displayed here, and $32,000 in prize money, which he gave to his first wife to support their sons.

an almost fanatical love of justice and the desire for personal independence—these are the features of the Jewish tradition which make me thank my stars that I belong to it." He also became involved with Zionism, the political movement to establish a Jewish national homeland in Palestine. (The nation of Israel was established as this homeland in 1948.)

In 1921 Einstein accepted an invitation from Zionist leader Chaim Weizmann to tour the United States to help raise money for the Hebrew University in Jerusalem, a school especially for Jewish students. Americans welcomed the scientist and his wife with great enthusiasm. Thousands of fans waited at the dock in New York to greet his ship, and he soon found himself mobbed by eager reporters and photographers. Dubbed the "Poet in Science" by the *New York Times*, Einstein lectured about relativity around the country and was a big hit at fund-raising events. Crowds flocked to catch a glimpse of him wherever he went. When he visited Washington, D.C., President Warren Harding received him at the White House.

Einstein had mixed feelings about all the attention he got in America. In a letter to a friend, he wrote that he had let himself "be shown around like a prize-winning ox." But then he noted that "now it's over and what remains is the pleasant awareness that I've accomplished something really worthwhile and that I fought bravely for the Jewish cause."

Over the next decade, Einstein was in great demand as a speaker. He traveled the world giving scientific lectures. He also began to contribute more of his time to causes close to his heart. He gave interviews and speeches and wrote articles on pacifism, peace, freedom, Zionism, and human rights. He felt a duty to use his fame to help make the world a better place.

While he was on his way to a lecture tour in Japan in 1922, Einstein learned that he had been awarded the 1921 Nobel Prize for Physics "for his service to theoretical physics and in particular for his discovery of the law of the photoelectric effect." Relativity was not mentioned; the Nobel committee considered it too controversial. Einstein gave the $32,000 prize money to Mileva to support their sons. He had been so sure he would eventually win the prize that he had promised it to her as part of their divorce agreement.

Einstein strolls with his good friend quantum physicist Niels Bohr. In response to Einstein's claim that "God doesn't play dice with the world," Bohr is said to have replied, "Stop telling God what to do!"

Einstein and Elsa enjoy a quiet moment in their Berlin apartment. "Music helps him when he is thinking about his theories," Elsa said about her husband. "He goes to his study, comes back, strikes a few chords on the piano, jots something down, returns to his study." Although she was devoted to Einstein and basked in his fame, she once confessed, "It is not ideal to be the wife of a genius. Your life ... seems to belong to everyone else."

"In the past it never occurred to me that every casual remark of mine would be snatched up and recorded. Otherwise I would have crept further into my shell."

"My pacifism is an instinctive feeling, a feeling that possesses me because the murder of people is disgusting. My attitude is not derived from any intellectual theory but is based on my deepest antipathy to every kind of cruelty and hatred."

Standing at a flag-covered podium, Einstein gives a speech in Pasadena, California, in 1931. At this time Einstein still supported pacifism. A few years later he reluctantly concluded that the only way to defeat the Nazis was by fighting them. In the background is a letter Einstein co-authored to President Roosevelt in 1939, alerting him that the Nazis might be developing an atomic bomb.

Despite his busy schedule and commitments to various causes, Einstein did not neglect his first love—physics. To him the world was a "great eternal riddle," and his strongest passion was to try to solve it. He sensed, however, that his greatest scientific achievements were behind him. In 1921 he wrote to a friend, "Discovery in the grand manner is for young people...and hence for me a thing of the past."

Nonetheless, Einstein made many more contributions to science in his lifetime. Between 1916 and 1925 he added several key ideas to the new science of quantum physics. Einstein had opened the way to quantum physics in 1905 with his pioneering article on the photoelectric effect. Since then the science had developed rapidly. In 1925 a new view of quantum theory, called quantum mechanics, emerged in the field of physics.

According to quantum mechanics, subatomic particles such as electrons do not have a definite position and speed, so their behavior cannot be precisely predicted. Einstein was disturbed by this lack of certainty, which he compared to God playing dice. He wrote, "It is hard to sneak a look at God's cards. But that he would choose to play dice with the world...is something I cannot believe for a single moment."

Einstein never was able to accept quantum mechanics. For nearly 30 years he debated the theory with his friend Niels Bohr, a Danish physicist who was a strong advocate of quantum mechanics. The objections Einstein raised helped Bohr and other physicists refine and strengthen the theory, which is now a central and essential part of physics.

In the 1920s Einstein also began a brand new scientific quest. He wanted to connect electromagnetism, gravity, space, and time all together in one broad mathematical theory, which he called the "unified field theory." He continued the search for the rest of his life. Many scientists thought he was wasting his time. Not Einstein. He believed that even if he did not succeed, one day someone else would.

Nazi party founder Adolf Hitler *(at the foot of the stairs)* ruled Germany from 1933 to 1945. During that time he supervised the murder of six million Jews.

In December 1930 Albert and Elsa Einstein spent the winter in California. Einstein had been invited to be a visiting professor at the California Institute of Technology (Caltech) in Pasadena. Once again he was hounded by the press upon arrival. "Swarms of reporters boarded the ship," he wrote in his travel diary. "An army of photographers...pounced on me liked starved wolves." Everyone wanted to meet the famous scientist, including one of the greatest movie stars of the time, Charlie Chaplin. Einstein enjoyed Pasadena, which he said was "like paradise....Always sunshine and fresh air, gardens with palm and pepper trees, and friendly people who smile at one and ask for autographs." He and Elsa returned to Caltech the following two winters.

Meanwhile in Germany the Nazi party, which was violently anti-Jewish, was growing more powerful by the day. In January 1933 the Nazis, led by party founder Adolf Hitler, took over the government. Einstein was in California when he heard the news. He knew that it would be very dangerous for him to go back to Germany. He was a Jew, and that alone put his life at risk. Moreover, he had spoken out strongly against the Nazis and in defense of democracy and pacifism. In addition, his property had been seized, his bank account frozen, and copies of his book on relativity burned in public. Einstein announced that he would not return to Germany. A German newspaper responded: "Good news from Einstein—he's not coming back." And he didn't. Einstein never set foot in Germany again.

Albert and Elsa left the United States in March 1933 and spent six months in Belgium and other European countries. During this time, Einstein faced a dilemma. As a pacifist, he was against war under any circumstances. But the Nazis were such a great threat to the freedom of Europe that they had to be defeated. With a heavy heart he concluded, "Organized power can be opposed only by organized power. Much as I regret this, there is no other way." Fighting the Nazis, he decided, was the lesser of two evils.

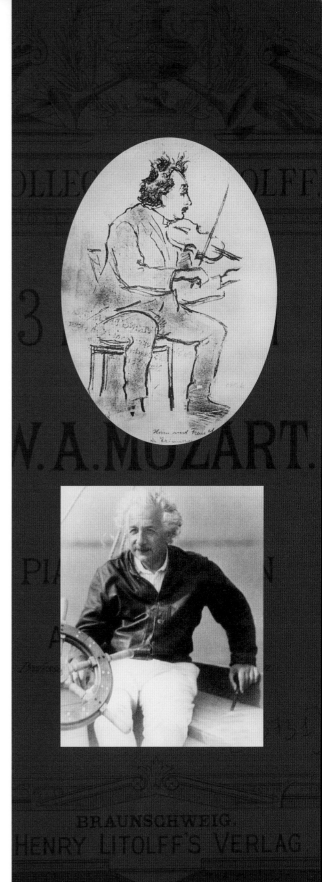

This sketch of Einstein playing the violin is set against a Mozart score that belonged to him. Einstein said music gave him "the highest possible degree of happiness." He also enjoyed sailing.

SATURDAY
MORNING,

Pittsburgh Po

 criptions
ing
6100.

Constantly Expressive—Einstein Wa

Einstein's ideas and opinions made front-page news after he talked to reporters about atomic energy in December 1934. Many Americans considered Einstein the ultimate authority on all scientific matters.

Professor Albert Einstein in a group of characteristic expressions, all moving slowly toward his famous smile in which his face actually lights up as he replies to the questions of his interviewers.

These portrait photographs, taken yesterday newspapermen who crowded around him, eagerly; next, getting a gleam of insight int

ION

t-Gazette

DECEMBER
29, 1934.

SPORTS, FINANCIAL,

CLASSIFIED SECTION

Up to His Subject

—Post-Gazette Photo.

swered the 20 first, listening estion; third, explaining slowly and patiently; fourth, making his point clear; and last—the smile itself. He did not hesitate to say, "I don't know," frequently in reply to queries by his interviewers.

ATOM ENERGY HOPE IS SPIKED BY EINSTEIN

Efforts at Loosing Vast Force Is Called Fruitless.

SAVANT TALKS HERE

Now Indicates Doubt Of Relativity Theory He Made Famous.

Blind chance, or cause and effect—which ever you prefer—may run the universe!

Space may be infinite, or it may be finite, nobody knows!

It may be curved, or not curved, just as you please!

Whatever you decide, no one can contradict you, because no one has so far been able to prove any one of these contentions. Still, you may be wrong, because some of the contentions may be proved in the future.

That is the contention of Prof. Albert Einstein.

But the "energy of the atom" is something else again. If you believe that man will someday be able to harness this boundless energy—to drive a great steamship across the ocean on a pint of water, for instance—then, according to Einstein, you are wrong now.

Energy of Atom.

The idea that man might some day utilize the atom's energy brought the only emphatic denial from the noted scientist yesterday when he was interviewed by a score of newspapermen at the

In October 1933 the Einsteins sailed for America with Albert's secretary, Helen Dukas. They settled in Princeton, New Jersey, where Einstein had already accepted a position at the Institute for Advanced Study—one of many institutions competing for the honor of having the great scientist join their staff. Elsa's daughter Margot joined them in Princeton the following year.

It didn't take long for Einstein to settle down in the little town. People made a fuss over him at first, but his presence was soon taken more or less for granted, and he was able to carry on with his work. His quest for a unified field theory still played a major role in his life. In his spare time, he played his violin with friends, and he sailed, another favorite hobby. He walked to and from his office at the institute, and he often stopped to chat with children and babble with babies along the way. According to one story, Einstein even helped a neighborhood child with her math homework. Children were fascinated by the friendly scientist's messy mass of white hair, his rumpled clothes, and the fact that he didn't wear socks. When some small boys asked why not, he is said to have answered, "I've reached an age when if somebody tells me to wear socks, I don't have to."

Although his life in Princeton was peaceful enough, Einstein was deeply concerned about the situation in Europe. He continued to speak out against the Nazis; he helped raise money for refugee children; he tried to help refugees obtain visas to enter the United States or other safe countries; and he helped found a group to resettle Jews and other refugees fleeing from Nazi terror. Among the refugees he helped come to America was a young photographer named Philippe Halsman, whose picture of Einstein would grace the cover of *Time* magazine's final issue of the 20th century.

In 1936 Elsa Einstein died after a long, painful battle with heart and kidney disease. Albert buried himself deeper in his work. Meanwhile Europe edged ever closer to war. In August 1939 Einstein learned from Hungarian-born physicist Leo Szilard that Nazi scientists might be developing an atomic bomb. He and Szilard then drafted a letter to President

"As long as I have any choice in the matter, I will live only in a country where civil liberty, tolerance and equality of all citizens before the law are the rule."

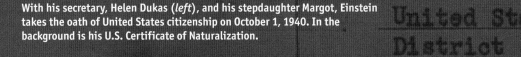

With his secretary, Helen Dukas (*left*), and his stepdaughter Margot, Einstein takes the oath of United States citizenship on October 1, 1940. In the background is his U.S. Certificate of Naturalization.

At his home in Princeton, Einstein shares a smile with Israeli Prime Minister David Ben-Gurion. In 1952 Ben-Gurion offered Einstein the presidency of the nation of Israel. It was largely an honorary office, but Einstein nonetheless politely declined.

Franklin Roosevelt. Einstein signed the letter, which alerted Roosevelt to the threat and urged him to start an American nuclear weapons research program. The following month Germany invaded Poland, and World War II began.

Historians debate whether Einstein's letter actually influenced Roosevelt. The U.S. effort to build an atomic bomb, known as the Manhattan Project, started in 1941. Einstein was not involved. Although he had become a U.S. citizen in 1940, his support of pacifism made him a security risk in the eyes of some members of the government. An FBI report stated that: "In view of his radical background, this office would not recommend the employment of Dr. Einstein, on matters of a secret nature." The FBI went on to collect a huge file on Einstein's political activities over the next 14 years.

In August 1945 the United States dropped atomic bombs on the Japanese cities of Hiroshima and Nagasaki. World War II ended shortly afterward. Einstein was so horrified that the bombs had targeted civilians that he later said he regretted having sent the letter to Roosevelt. And he was relieved that he could truthfully say, "I have done no work on the atomic bomb, no work at all." Einstein realized the threat that nuclear weapons posed to humanity, and for the rest of his life he was involved in efforts to prevent nuclear warfare.

After the war Einstein refused to renew his ties with the German scientific community. "The Germans have slaughtered my Jewish brethren," he said, referring to the mass murder of Jews during the Holocaust. "I will have nothing further to do with the Germans."

He continued to live in Princeton with Margot, his secretary Helen Dukas, and his sister Maja, who had come there in 1939. Still active in science, he kept plugging away at equations for his unified field theory even after he retired from the Institute for Advanced Study in 1945. Keeping in touch with his friends and colleagues all over the world took up many hours. Just going through the daily mail was time consuming. By now Einstein was a living legend. He received thousands of letters from strangers seeking advice and opinions from "the world's smartest man." A great number of these letters were from children, and he replied to many of them.

Maja died in 1951, five years after a stroke left her bedridden. "During the last years I read to her every evening from the finest books of old and new literature," Einstein wrote to a cousin. "Now I miss her more than one can imagine."

In 1952 the nation of Israel, recently created as a Jewish homeland, asked Einstein to become its president after the death of its first president, Einstein's old friend Chaim Weizmann. Einstein was deeply touched, but he turned the offer down. In his response he stated, "I am deeply moved by the offer from our State of Israel, and at once saddened and ashamed that I cannot accept it....[My] relationship to the Jewish

Deep in thought, Einstein pauses amid the clutter of his office in Princeton. The scientist stayed active in peace efforts and his beloved physics until the very end of his life.

people has become my strongest human bond, ever since I became fully aware of our precarious situation among the nations of the world."

Einstein's health began to fail in the last years of his life, but he stayed active in the causes dear to him. He continued to campaign against the buildup of nuclear weapons and to advocate world peace and international cooperation. He delivered talks and gave interviews on these subjects for radio and television broadcasts. He also supported the emerging African-American civil rights movement in the United States.

Although Einstein loved and admired the United States, he was not shy about criticizing his new homeland when he believed it was on the wrong track. When Senator Joseph McCarthy and his House Un-American Activities Committee began branding people as Communists and destroying their careers and lives in the early 1950s, Einstein was one of the first public figures to speak up against this mistreatment. To him McCarthy's proceedings were a threat to intellectual freedom and to democracy itself. He argued in 1954, "The current investigations are...[a] greater danger to our society than those few Communists in the country ever could be."

In his later years Einstein gave up playing his beloved violin. "I am done with fiddling," he wrote to a friend. "With the passage of years, it has become more and more unbearable for me to listen to my own playing.... What has remained is the relentless work on difficult scientific problems. The fascinating magic of that work will continue to my last breath."

On April 16, 1955, Albert Einstein was admitted to Princeton Hospital with a rupture of an aneurysm of the abdominal aorta—basically a burst blood vessel in his abdomen. According to his friends and family, he faced death calmly and untroubled. On April 18, 1955, the world's most famous scientist died. He was 76 years old. According to his wishes, there was no funeral service. His body was cremated, and his ashes were scattered at a place kept secret to this day.

"The important thing is not to stop questioning.
Curiosity has its own reason for existing.
One cannot help but be in awe when
one contemplates the mysteries of eternity."

Lecturing at Caltech in 1931, Albert Einstein writes a
gravity-related equation on the blackboard.

AFTERWORD

Albert Einstein became a worldwide celebrity when his general theory of relativity was confirmed in 1919. Newspapers, magazines, and later on movie newsreels and television spread his image and ideas around the globe to a curious public. People wanted to know all about the eccentric but charming scientist who had upended traditional notions of time and space. Soon Einstein was as famous as top athletes and movie stars are now. His very name became a synonym for genius.

Today, a half century after his death, Einstein is still incredibly popular. His name and face are instantly recognized, and advertisers have used them to sell everything from candy to cola, from cameras to computers. Einstein's shaggy-haired image also appears on all kinds of merchandise, including posters, T-shirts, mugs, Halloween masks, and even bobble-head dolls.

Einstein's current popularity, however, is based on far more than his commercial appeal. Curiosity about his life and his science remains stronger than ever. Hundreds of books and magazine articles have been written about him and his theories in recent years, and he is the subject of scores of Web sites. He has also been featured as a character in plays, movies, and operas. Indeed, Einstein has become a mythical figure, honored not only for his extraordinary brainpower but also for his deep commitment to making the world a better place.

In its final issue of 1999, *Time* magazine named Einstein "Person of the Century." The editors singled him out for the honor "in a century that will be remembered foremost for its science and technology." Certainly Einstein was the most important scientist of the 20th century, perhaps of all time. His special theory of relativity transformed human understanding of the universe and opened our imagination to all kinds of possibilities. It also opened the door to nuclear power plants and nuclear weapons. His work on the photoelectric effect contributed to the birth of quantum physics, which is the ultimate basis for all of modern electronics, including computers and cell phones. Quantum physics also laid the foundation for lasers and their many applications, including barcode scanners, CD players, laser surgery, and fiber-optic communication lines.

Einstein's office at Princeton's Institute for Advanced Study on the day of his death.

Einstein's crowning glory, his general theory of relativity, eventually led physicists to the Big Bang theory of the formation of the universe. It also gives astronomers the tools they need to understand such mysterious objects in space as black holes, quasars, and pulsars—all of which were detected after Einstein's death. General relativity also figures in life on Earth: For example, the global positioning system (GPS) uses Einstein's equations to correct for the effects of gravity and speed.

Einstein spent the last 30 years or so of his life in the unsuccessful pursuit of a unified field theory—one simple theory that could explain all the laws of physics. Some of his contemporaries considered this work a waste of time. But now it seems that Einstein was actually a couple of generations ahead of his time. Today, one of the hottest topics in physics is the search for a "theory of everything."

In 1949 Albert Einstein wrote that his scientific work was "motivated by an irresistible longing to understand the secrets of nature." Thanks to his dazzling discoveries, at least some of those secrets have been revealed to us all.

CHRONOLOGY

A gargoyle at Caltech of Einstein with his violin.

March 14, 1879
Albert Einstein is born in Ulm, Germany.

1880
Einstein family moves to Munich.

November 18, 1881
Albert's sister, Maja, is born.

1894
Einstein family moves to Milan, Italy. Albert is left in Munich to finish school.

1895
Einstein quits school in Munich and joins his family in Milan. Attends high school in Aarau, Switzerland.

1896
Renounces German citizenship. Enrolls at the Swiss Federal Institute of Technology (the Polytechnic).

1900
Graduates from the Polytechnic.

1901
Becomes a Swiss citizen.

1902
Takes a job with the Swiss patent office in Bern.

January 6, 1903
Marries Mileva Maric.

1905
Einstein's *annus mirabilis*. He publishes four articles that revolutionize science, including two on his special theory of relativity. Formulates the equation "$E=mc^2$."

1909
Einstein resigns from patent office and takes a job as professor of physics at University of Zurich.

1914
Accepts research position at University of Berlin. Separates from Mileva, who returns to Switzerland with their two sons.

1915
Einstein completes general theory of relativity.

1919
Marries Elsa Loewenthal. General theory of relativity confirmed by British astronomers. Einstein becomes world famous.

1922
Awarded the 1921 Nobel Prize in physics.

1930–1932
Spends three winters as visiting professor at California Institute of Technology.

1933
Nazis come to power in Germany. Einstein and Elsa emigrate to the United States and settle in Princeton, New Jersey.

1936
Elsa Einstein dies.

1939
Einstein co-authors and signs letter to President Franklin D. Roosevelt urging the United States to research nuclear weapons.

1940
Einstein becomes a U.S. citizen.

1952
Einstein is offered presidency of Israel; declines.

April 18, 1955
Albert Einstein dies at age 76 from a ruptured aortic aneurysm.

DEAR MR. EINSTEIN
I AM A LITTLE GIRL OF SIX.
I SAW YOUR PICTURE IN THE PAPER. I THINK YOU OUGHT TO HAVE YOUR HAIRCUT, SO YOU CAN LOOK BETTER.
CORDIALLY YOURS,
ANN G. KOCIN.

A letter from a young admirer.

RESOURCES

There's a mind-boggling amount of information about Albert Einstein. Here are the resources I found most helpful:

BOOKS

Bartusiak, Marcia. *Einstein's Unfinished Symphony: Listening to the Sounds of Space-Time.* Washington, D.C.: Joseph Henry Press, 2000.

Bodanis, David. *E=mc²: A Biography of the World's Most Famous Equation.* New York: Walker & Company, 2000.

Bryson, Bill. *A Short History of Nearly Everything.* New York: Broadway Books, 2003.

Clark, Ronald W. *Einstein: The Life and Times.* New York: Avon Books, 1984.

Dukas, Helen, and **Banesh Hoffman.** *Albert Einstein: The Human Side.* Princeton, NJ: Princeton University Press, 1989.

Einstein, Albert. *Dear Professor Einstein: Albert Einstein's Letters to and from Children.* Edited by Alice Calaprice. Amherst, NY: Prometheus Books, 2002.

Einstein, Albert. *Einstein on Peace.* Edited by Otto Nathan and Heinz Norden. New York: Simon & Schuster, 1960.

Einstein, Albert. *The Expanded Quotable Einstein.* Collected and edited by Alice Calaprice. Princeton, NJ: Princeton University Press, 2000.

Einstein, Albert. *Ideas and Opinions.* New York: Wings Books, no date.

Gribbin, John. *Almost Everyone's Guide to Science.* New Haven, CT: Yale University Press, 1998.

Gribbin, Mary, and John Gribbin. *Time & Space.* New York: DK Publishing, Inc., 1994.

Hoffman, Banesh. *Albert Einstein: Creator & Rebel.* New York: Penguin Books, 1972.

Overbye, Dennis. *Einstein in Love: A Scientific Romance.* New York: Viking, 2000.

Pais, Abraham. *'Subtle is the Lord...': The Science and the Life of Albert Einstein.* New York: Oxford University Press, 1982.

Rosenkranz, Ze'ev. *The Einstein Scrapbook.* Baltimore, MD: Johns Hopkins University Press, 2002.

Sayen, Jamie. *Einstein in America: The Scientist's Conscience in the Age of Hitler and Hiroshima.* New York: Crown Publishers, Inc., 1985.

Severance, John B. *Einstein: Visionary Scientist.* New York: Clarion Books, 1999.

Suplee, Curt. *Milestones of Science.* Washington, D.C.: National Geographic Society, 2000.

White, Michael, and John Gribbin. *Einstein: A Life in Science.* New York: Dutton, 1994.

NEWSPAPER

Washington Post: October 29, 2003, February 21, 2004, March 11, 2004.

VIDEO

Einstein Revealed. NOVA. WGBH Video. 1996.

WEB SITES

Albert Einstein Archives. The Hebrew University of Jerusalem
www.albert-einstein.org/.index.html

Einstein. American Museum of Natural History
www.amnh.org/exhibitions/einstein/

Einstein: Image and Impact. Center for History of Physics, American Institute of Physics (AIP)
www.aip.org/history/einstein/

Einstein Revealed. NOVA Online
www.pbs.org/wgbh/nova/einstein/index.html

THE *TIME* 100. Person of the Century: Albert Einstein
www.time.com/time/time100/poc/magazine/albert_einstein5a.html

Way to Go, Einstein. Ology, American Museum of Natural History.
www.ology.amnh.org/einstein/index.html

Time magazine, December 31, 1999.

CREDITS

QUOTE SOURCES

Quotations from Albert Einstein and others are taken from the following sources, which are fully cited on page 62. Primary source information provided by the Albert Einstein Archives.

"One thing I have learned..." Page 5: *Albert Einstein: Creator & Rebel,* by Banesh Hoffmann, p. v (Primary source: Letter to Hans Muehsam July 9, 1951, AEA, 38-408); Page 8: "I have no special..." *The Expanded Quotable Einstein,* edited by Alice Calaprice (*EQE*), p. 16 (Primary source: Letter to Carl Seelig, March 11, 1952, AEA, 39-013); "exceedingly friendly..." *Einstein: The Life and Times,* by Ronald W. Clark, p. 22; Page 9: "When I was a little boy.." *Albert Einstein: The Human Side,* by Helen Dukas and Banesh Hoffmann, p. 19; (Primary source: letter to S. Bloom, May 26, 1936); Page 10: "My parents were..." *EQE*, p. 18 (Primary source: CPAE, vol. 1, Biographical sketch, Albert Einstein, by Maja Winteler-Einstein); "Where are its wheels?" *EQE*, p. 47 (Primary source: CPAE, vol 1, Biographical sketch, Albert Einstein, by Maja Winteler-Einstein); Page 11: "it takes a sound skull..." *E=mc²*, by David Bodanis, p. 87 (Primary source: CPAE, vol 1, Biographical sketch, Albert Einstein, by Maja Winteler-Einstein); "really began to learn..." Hoffmann, p. 20; Page 12: "I can still remember ..." *Einstein: A Life in Science,* by Michael White and John Gribbin, p. 10; (Primary source: Albert Einstein, Autobiographical Notes, 1949) Page 13: "Yesterday Albert got..." White and Gribbin, p. 11 (Primary source: CPAE vol. 1, Letter by Pauline Einstein to Fanny Einstein); "To me the worst..." *EQE*, p. 69 (Primary source: Address given at Albany, October 15, 1936); Page 14: "breathless attention" Hoffmann, p. 24 (Primary source: Albert Einstein, Autobiographical Notes 1949); Page 15: "dull, mechanized method..." Hoffmann, p. 25; Page 16: "the over-empha-sized..." Hoffmann, p. 26; "sure of himself" and "unhampered by convention" *Einstein in Love: A Scientific Romance,* by Dennis Overbye, p. 13; "fire...in his playing" *Einstein in America,* by Jamie Sayen, p. 30; Page 17: Sayen, p. 29 (Primary source: Letter to E. Marangoni, August 16, 1946); Page 19: *EQE*, p. 226; Page 20: "thought experiment" *'Subtle is the Lord...',* by Abraham Pais, p. 131; "a freedom which I" Pais, p. 44 (Primary source: Albert Einstein, Autobiographical Notes, 1949); Page 21: "cram all this stuff" and "I found the consideration..." Hoffmann, p. 31 (Primary source: Albert Einstein, Autobiographical Notes, 1949); "From what people..." Hoffmann, p. 32 (Primary source: Letter to A. Stern, May 3, 1901); Page 22: Overbye, p. 62 (Primary source: CPAE vol. 1); Page 23: "Well, now I am..." Overbye, p. 105 (Primary source: letter to M. Besso, January 22, 1903); "sitting...in front of a heap..." Clark, p. 84; Page 30: *EQE*, p. 10; Page 30: "Imagination is more important than knowledge. Knowledge is limited, imagination encircles the world." Quoted in interview with G.S. Viereck, October 26, 1929) Page 31: *EQE*, p. 236; Page 32: Clark, p. 27; Page 33: *EQE*, p. 327; Page 34: *Einstein: Image and Impact,* American Institute of Physics (AIP) Web site, www.aip.org/history/

einstein/early4.htm; Page 35: "send me news..." *EQE,* p. 32 (Primary source: Letter to Mileva, July, 1914, CPAE, Vol. 8, Doc. 23); "little bears" White and Gribbin, p. 110; Page 36: Hoffmann, p. 116; Page 37: "I have just completed..." AIP Web site, www.aip.org/history/einstein/great2.htm (Primary source: Letter to Hans Albert, November 4, 1915, CPAE vol. 8, doc. 134); "I was sitting..." *EQE,* p. 242 (In Kyoto, Japan lecture December 14, English translation by Y.A. Ono); "Every step..." Pais, p. 210 (Primary source: Letter to M. Besso, March 26, 1912, AEA 7-066); Page 41: "flooded with questions..." AIP Web site, www.aip.org/history/einstein/fame2.htm; "Just as with..." *EQE,* p. 8 (Primary source: Letter to Max Born, September 9, 1920 AEA 8-151); "At present every..." *EQE,* p. 238 (Primary source: Letter to Marcel Grossmann, September 12, 1920 AEA 11-499); "The pursuit of knowledge..." *Ideas and Opinions,* by Albert Einstein, p. 185; Page 42: "be shown around..." *The Einstein Scrapbook,* by Ze'ev Rosenkranz, p. 117 (Primary source: Letter to Michel Besso, May 28, 1921 AEA 7-335); Page 43: "now it's over and..." Rosenkranz, p. 117 (Primary source: Letter to Michel Besso, May 28, 1921 AEA 7-335); Page 43: "great eternal riddle" *EQE,* p. 220 (Primary source: Albert Einstein, Autobiographical Notes, 1949); "Discovery in the..." Hoffmann, p. 222; "God doesn't play dice..." and "Stop telling God..." *EQE,* pp. 251-252; Page 44: "Music helps him..." Pais, p. 301; "It is not ideal..." *EQE,* pp. 328-329; Page 45: *EQE,* p. 17 (Primary source: To Carl Seelig, October 25, 1953 AEA 39-053); Page 46: "My Pacifism is an instinctive feeling.." *EQE,* p. 163 (Primary source: To Paul Hutchinson, July 1929); Page 47: "It is hard to sneak..." *EQE,* p. 245 (Primary source: Letter to C. Lanczos, March 21, 1942); "Swarms of reporters..." Rosenkranz, p. 175 (Primary source: Travel Diary, December 11, 1930); Page 48: "like paradise..." *EQE,* (Primary source: Letter to Lebach family, January 16, 1931 AEA, 47-373) p. 53; Page 49: "Organized power..." *EQE,* p. 174; "the highest possible..." Rosenkranz, p. 142 (Primary source: Quoted in an interview with G.S. Viereck, October 26, 1929); Page 52: Sayen, p. 69; Page 53: *EQE,* p. 190; Page 54: Bodanis, p. 130; Page 55: "I have done no..." *EQE,* p. 174; "The Germans have..." *EQE,* p. 237; "During the last years..." Hoffmann, p. 242; "I am deeply moved..." Rosenkranz, p. 103 (Primary source: Letter to State of Israel, November 18, 1952); Page 56: "The current investigations..." *EQE,* p. 197 (Primary source: Letter to Arnold, March 1954); "I am done..." Hoffmann, p. 244; Page 57: AIP Web site, www.aip.org/history/einstein/ae77.htm (Primary source: Letter to Queen Elisabeth of the Belgians, January 6, 1951); Page 60: "motivated by,,," *EQE,* p. 16; Back cover: "The pursuit of truth and beauty is a sphere..." (Primary source: Aphorism written for Adriana Enriques, October, 1921 AEA, 36-588).

ILLUSTRATIONS CREDITS

FRONT COVER PHOTOGRAPH (Einstein): Courtesy of the Albert Einstein Archives, the Jewish National & University Library, the Hebrew University of Jerusalem, Israel.

FRONT AND BACK COVER PHOTOGRAPH (manuscript): © The Hebrew University of Jerusalem.

BACK COVER PHOTOGRAPH (inset): Bettmann/CORBIS

All images, except as noted below, are courtesy of the Albert Einstein Archives, Jewish National & University Library, Hebrew University of Jerusalem.

Artwork on pages 29 and 38 by Stuart Armstrong.

1, AP/Wide World Photos; 2-3, Estrellit Karsch/Retna; 5, California Institute of Technology; 6 (inset), © Philippe Halsman Studio; 11 (background), CORBIS; 12, City Archive, Ulm; 17, Jose Fuste Raga/CORBIS; 18-19 (background), Matt Brown/CORBIS; 18-19 (inset), Image Archive ETH-Bibliothek, Zurich; 21 (lower), Image Archive ETH-Bibliothek, Zurich; 22 (background), EINSTEIN, ALBERT: THE COLLECTED PAPERS OF ALBERT EINSTEIN. Princeton University Press. Reprinted by permission of Princeton University Press; 22 (inset), Image Archive ETH-Bibliothek, Zurich; 24, CORBIS; 25, CORBIS; 26 (left), American Institute of Physics; 26 (right), American Institute of Physics; 26-27, Getty Images; 27 (left), American Institute of Physics; 27 (right), American Institute of Physics; 30, E. O.Hoppe/Mansell/Time Life Pictures/Getty Images; 32-33, AP/Wide World Photos; 33, CORBIS; 34, California Institute of Technology; 36 (inset), Lick Observatory; 39, Topical Press Agency/Getty Images; 40 (background), *The New York Times;* 40 (upper left, inset), Brown Brothers; 40 (lower left, inset), *The New York Times;* 40 (right, inset), THE GRANGER COLLECTION, New York; 42 (left) © The Nobel Foundation; 43, CORBIS; 44-45, Keystone/Getty Images; 46, Bettmann/CORBIS; 47 (upper, inset), Emil Orlik, courtesy Albert Einstein Archives, Hebrew University of Jerusalem; 47 (lower, inset), American Institute of Physics; 48 (background), MPI/Getty Images; 48 (inset), California Institute of Technology; 50-51, American Institute of Physics; 53 (inset), American Stock/Getty Images; 54, Bettmann/CORBIS; 57, Ernst Haas/Getty Images; 58, Bettmann/CORBIS; 60, Ralph Morse/Time Life Pictures/Getty Images; 61 (upper), California Institute of Technology; 62, Time Life Pictures/*Time* Magazine, copyright © Time Inc./Time Life Pictures/Getty Images.

INDEX

One of the world's largest nonprofit scientific and educational organizations, the National Geographic Society was founded in 1888 "for the increase and diffusion of geographic knowledge." Fulfilling this mission, the Society educates and inspires millions every day through its magazines, books, television programs, videos, maps and atlases, research grants, the National Geographic Bee, teacher workshops, and innovative classroom materials. The Society is supported through membership dues, charitable gifts, and income from the sale of its educational products. This support is vital to National Geographic's mission to increase global understanding and promote conservation of our planet through exploration, research, and education.

For more information, please call 1-800-NGS LINE (647-5463) or write to the following address:

NATIONAL GEOGRAPHIC SOCIETY
1145 17th Street N.W.
Washington, D.C. 20036-4688
U.S.A.

Visit the Society's Web site:
www.nationalgeographic.com